THE SCOTT FORESMAN EXERCISE BOOK

Revised by

Joel Henderson

Chattanooga State Technical Community College

Upper Saddle River, New Jersey 07458

© 2008 by PEARSON EDUCATION, INC.
Upper Saddle River, New Jersey 07458

10 9 8 7 6 5 4 3 2 1

ISBN 10: 0-13-233456-9
ISBN 13: 978-0-13-233456-3

Printed in the United States of America

Contents

SHAPING LANGUAGE

UNDERSTANDING GRAMMAR

UNDERSTANDING PUNCTUATION AND MECHANICS

Preface

The 100 exercises in this book give students a chance to try out what they have learned from any text in the *Scott Foresman* series. The exercises cover aspects of style, grammar, and punctuation and mechanics, some devoted to particular ESL problems. With a few exceptions, the work can be completed on the pages of this book. Many of the exercises are in connected discourse, with passages on cross-disciplinary topics.

Each exercise is keyed to the relevant section in Scott Foresman *Handbook (SFHBB)*, *SF Writer (SFW)*, and *SF Compact (SFC)*, as in this sample exercise heading:

Exercise 1   **SFHB 15a**
Levels of Language   **SFW 8b**
                                                                         SFC 5b

Students who have difficulty with any exercise should read the appropriate text explanation and then try again to complete the exercise.

Most exercises have a sample answer in the back of the book to assist instructors in discussing exercises with students and to help students who are working independently. All suggested answers appear in a separate answer key, which instructors may access from the Instructor Resource Center located at *www.prenhall.com*.

Answers are labeled "possible" when the corresponding exercises encourage choice in responding. In these cases, the answers given are suggestions. Even for the objective exercises, usage is often flexible and some users may have variant answers. The answers given conform to the usage recommended in the *Scott Foresman* series.

SHAPING LANGUAGE

Exercise 1   *SFHB 15a*
Levels of Language   *SFW 8b*
                                                SFC 5b

What level of formality do you think would be appropriate for writing in each of these situations? In each case, consider what impression the writer wants to make and how much distance he or she would want to maintain between reader and writer. Give reasons for your choice.

1.   A letter to a representative or senator asking to be considered for a summer internship in his or her office.

2.   A brochure recruiting people to work on a house being constructed by Habitat for Humanity.

3.   A column in your weekly church newsletter that recounts noteworthy activities by or recognition of members of the church.

4.   A short biographical sketch for your personal Web page.

Find and clip a syndicated newspaper column such as those written by
George Will, William Safire, Molly Ivins, or William Raspberry.
Underline words and phrases with strong negative or positive
connotations. Then clip a news story from the same paper and do the
same. Discuss any differences in how the two pieces handle connotative
language.

Rewrite the following sentences to eliminate sexist language or implications.

1. Women in their forties and fifties who want to look their best often consider cosmetic surgery.

2. Today even a high school physics teacher should know his astrophysics, or he'll look out of date to his students.

3. The hospital's new series of nutrition workshops appeals to mothers concerned about their children's health.

4. Businesswomen often worry about leaving their children in day care while working long hours to get ahead.

5. The lady running for Congress in my district has been a county judge for many years.

Working in a group, decide which of these sentences have hints of offensive bias (some of them certainly arguable). Which might be acceptable in some circumstances? How could you change those that are not?

1.   The chemistry professor was impressed to see that most of the girls in his advanced course had scored high marks on the exam.

2.   Barney Frank, who is almost the only open homosexual in the U.S. Congress, represents a district in Massachusetts.

3.   Although Betty Friedan is over seventy, she still writes extensively and travels widely.

4.   The hospice is looking for volunteers to help AIDS victims with household tasks and grocery shopping.

5.   Many Americans were unaware that President Franklin Delano Roosevelt was crippled, since he was rarely photographed in his wheelchair during public appearances.

Which of these sentences might alienate a reader sensitive to bias?
Which ones should be changed? Why or why not? What changes would
you suggest?

1. The cops used poor judgment about gathering evidence at the
   crime scene.

2. Welfare mothers have become the target of budget-conscious
   legislators who believe that hardworking taxpayers shouldn't
   have to support people who won't work.

3. That organization is known for attracting sorority girls and
   fraternity guys.

4. It's amazing that Jason became a successful lawyer, since he grew
   up in the inner-city ghetto, surrounded by poverty and despair.

Recast these sentences in agent/action patterns that show more clearly
who is doing what to whom. Break the sentences into shorter ones if you
like.

1.   Raising $3 million to renovate the drama facilities on campus was
        the goal of Lincoln Brown, the new college president.

2.   The experience of playing Horatio in a college production of
        Hamlet had been influential in convincing President Brown of the
        value of the performing arts.

3.   Helping President Brown to convince wealthy donors that
        restoring and expanding the old theater was a good idea was a
        small group of actors, all of them alumni of the school.

4.   An unexpected donation of $1 million made by a prominent local
        banker who had once played Hamlet gave the actors and
        President Brown reason to celebrate.

Exercise 7
Avoiding Overloaded Subjects

SFHB 17a
SFW 10b
SFC16a

Rewrite the following sentences to simplify their overcrowded openings.

1. Among those who are unhappy about the lack of morality and
    standards in the television shows coming from Hollywood today
    and who would like to see pressure on producers for more
    responsible programming are activists from remarkably different
    political groups.

2. The elimination of hurtful gender, racial, and ethnic stereotypes,
    particularly from situation comedies, where they are sometimes a
    key element of the humor, is a key demand of political groups on
    the left.

3. TV's almost complete disregard of the role religion plays in the
    daily lives of most ordinary people, evident in the fact that so few
    sitcom characters ever go to church or pray, irritates groups on
    the political right.

4. Raising the specter of censorship and equating every attack on
    Hollywood to an assault on the First Amendment has been the
    quick response of many television producers to criticism of their
    products.

Exercise 8
Cutting to be *Verbs*

SFHB 17a
SFW 10a
SFC 16a

Replace the *to be* forms in these sentences with active and more lively verbs. The original verbs are boldfaced. (It may help if you make the agent a person or a concrete object.)

1. There **was** a protest among restaurateurs when the city decided to increase the number of health inspectors.

2. It **had been** the determination of city officials, however, that many restaurants were not in a state of compliance with local health ordinances.

3. The occurrence of rodent droppings in pantries and the storage of meat at incorrect temperatures **were** also matters of concern to several TV reporters.

4. It was the hope of both the politicians and the restaurateurs that there **would be** a quick solution to this embarrassing problem.

Exercise 9   *SFHB 17a*
Identifying Passive Verbs   *SFW 10a*
                 SFC 16a

Underline the passive verbs in the following sentences and then rewrite those that might be more readable as active verbs.

1. The writing of research papers is traditionally dreaded by students everywhere.

2. The negative attitudes can be changed by writers themselves if the assignments are regarded by them as opportunities to explore and improve their communities.

3. When conventional topics are chosen by researchers, apathy is likely to be experienced by them and their readers alike.

4. But if writers are encouraged to choose community-related topics that can be explored through books, articles, fieldwork, interviews, and online investigations, a better project will be produced.

Make the following sentences more readable by breaking them into more
manageable chunks.

1.   The job a young woman has in high school can play an important

        role in introducing her to new responsibilities, increasing her self-

        confidence, and getting her accustomed to the expectation that

        she will likely have to earn her own way through life and

        shouldn't anticipate that someone else, usually a man, will

        shoulder the burden of providing her security, shelter, or other

        necessities.

2.   Parents are often ambivalent about having their high school-aged

        children work because almost inevitably it causes a conflict

        between the demands of schoolwork and extracurricular activities

        (such as sports, civic clubs, debate teams, band) and the

        expectations of employers, a balance many high schoolers are

        simply not mature enough to handle on their own, often choosing

        the immediate material goods furnished by a job over the less

        obvious benefits afforded by a good education.

3.   Many parents, however, aware of the limitations of their own

        training in school, may believe that it is no more important to

        learn square roots, the capitals of Asian countries, or the metrics of Chaucer's poetry than it is to discover how tough it is to deal with customers, show up on time, manage other workers, or pay taxes, experiences that an after-school job will quickly give most teenagers, whose images of work are badly distorted by films and television.

Streamline and strengthen this paragraph from a student's first draft by cutting unnecessary generalizations or explanations and trimming at other places that seem wordy. You may need to cut or revise words, phrases, or whole sentences.

There are many different scholarly views concerning Alexander the Great's ultimate goal in relation to his military pursuits. Some historians consider Alexander to have been a power-hungry tyrant without whom the world would have been better off. Others see Alexander as the great unifier of humankind, one who attempted to bring together many cultures in one coherent empire. Others view him as the ultimate pragmatist—not necessarily having any preplanned goals and aspirations of conquering the world, but merely a king who made the very best of his existing circumstances. Some believe that Alexander's accomplishments were not great at all, but that most of what was written concerning Alexander is basically just a mixture of legend and myth. Others feel his achievements stand as monuments in human history to the enormous capability of the human spirit and will.

Revise the following sentences to eliminate the sprawling, wordy, or clichéd opening phrase.

1. On the occasion of the newspaper's seventy-fifth anniversary, the governor visited the editorial offices.

2. Regardless of the fact that I have revised the speech three times, I still don't like my conclusion.

3. In the modern American society in which we live today, many people still attend church regularly.

4. By virtue of the fact that flood insurance rates are so high, many people go uninsured, risking their property.

Rewrite the following sentences to reduce clutter by substituting single words for wordy phrases. Rearrange the sentences as necessary.

1. In the event that you are in proximity to Greene County this weekend, you should not miss the opportunity to visit the autumn Concours d'Elegance, an annual exhibit of classic cars.

2. There is the possibility that you may have the chance to touch and feel many quite unusual and different vehicles, from dowdy Edsels with gearshift buttons in the middle of their steering wheels to tiny Corvairs with air-cooled engines under louvered deck lids at the back.

3. However, don't expect to make an inspection of the more unique makes and the basically timeless art of such prestigious automakers as Bugatti, Duesenberg, or Hispano-Suiza.

4. Regardless of the fact that Greene County's show is a small show, you can take great satisfaction in examining quite handsome old Hudsons, Nashes, Jaguars, and Corvettes that are tended by owners who are willing and eager to talk about them at great length.

Change the boldfaced nominalizations to verbs that state the actions of the sentences, and make additional revisions as necessary.

1.   The registrar's note is a **clarification** of the school's admissions

      policy.

2.   It is a matter of substantial **disputation** among sociologists

      whether the **gentrification** of urban neighborhoods is a

      beneficial process to inner-city residents.

3.   The **utilization** of traditional phonics in more and more

      elementary reading classes is an **indication** that many teachers

      are feeling **dissatisfaction** with more contemporary approaches to

      language **instruction**.

4.   The systems analyst convinced us that the **connectivity** and

      interchangeability of our equipment gave our new computer

      system **enhanced potential**.

Exercise 15   *SFHB 17c*
Focusing Verbs on the Action   *SFW 10b*
                                                 SFC 16c

Revise the following sentences to condense long verb phrases into more
active expressions.

1.   Many people are of the opinion that the federal government has
        grown too large.

2.   An almost equal number of people hold the conviction that many
        citizens have need of services provided by federal programs.

3.   This difference in public opinion is indicative of the dilemma
        faced by many politicians today.

4.   Their constituents often are not in favor of paying for exactly the
        services which they have expectations of getting.

Rewrite the following sentences to reduce redundancy and wordiness.

1. I realized that if I were ever to reach law school, I would have to increase my competitiveness in the skill of written prose composition.

2. *Fraser* to me is a situation comedy-type show.

3. Many traits characterize a truly excellent student adviser, and one of the more important qualities, if not the most important quality of an adviser, is a lively personality.

4. I have often wondered if everyone's taste in toothpaste is the same and which brand is the most widely used of those brands of toothpaste that are most widely advertised.

Review the intensifiers in the following passage and cut any words or phrases you regard as unnecessary.

The Grand Canyon is a quite unique geological treasure in northwestern Arizona, basically formed by the relentless power of the Colorado River cutting a gorge for many, many eons through solid rock. Standing at the edge of the canyon is a totally awesome experience. The canyon walls drop far into the depths, thousands of feet, a seriously deep drop, exposing very different layers of limestone, sandstone, and volcanic rock. These really magnificent canyons recede into the distance like ancient castles, an absolutely remarkable panorama of color and shadow.

Exercise 18
Reducing the Number of Prepositional Phrases

SFHB 17c
SFW 10b
SFC 16c

Revise the following sentences to reduce the number of prepositional phrases where they make the sentences awkward or monotonous. Some sentences may require extensive revision.

1.   Patrick O'Brian is the author of one of the most popular series of novels about the history of the Royal Navy of Britain during the time of the Napoleonic wars.

2.   O'Brian's books focus on the lives of a genial captain by the name of Jack Aubrey and of a ship's surgeon by the name of Stephen Maturin who is also in the service of the secret intelligence of England.

3.   The novels cover a long period of history, focusing on a worldwide struggle for territory and for dominance in the early nineteenth century between the British people and the forces of Napoleon Bonaparte, the emperor of the French nation.

4.   In his love of the sea, in his fascination with the languages of the world, and in his professional interest in the world of espionage, Patrick O'Brian resembles his much loved heroes.

Draw a line through any relative pronouns (*who, whom, that, which*) that contribute to wordiness. Underline any such pronouns you regard as necessary for clarity.

1. Some of the people who might be willing to endure a little less environmental consciousness are parents of children whom environmentalists have turned into Green Police.

2. Third graders who used to read Harry Potter novels suddenly can't wait to locate "Tips to Save Our Planet" in the daily newspaper, which carries dozens of slick, unrecyclable inserts.

3. Full of moral superiority, youngsters who can barely read are circulating petitions that condemn industries that are polluting the air.

4. Shrewd are the parents who steer their children's activist impulses in productive directions by asking them to read supermarket labels and to find the items that are marked "Recyclable."

Underline the strategies the writer has used to unify the following paragraph: topic sentence, transition words, repetition, parallel structure, and so on. Identify the strategy in the space above your underlined words.

Day 1 set the tone for our really heavy driving days: We stopped only for gasoline and bathroom breaks, which usually coincided after 350 to 400 miles. We averaged about 70 mph for at least 14 hours. We ate what we had in the car or what we could get from travel plazas and gas stations. We didn't run the air conditioning, though we never talked about why. We didn't listen to the radio much because we had the windows down and could barely hear. We discussed—in shouts—whatever popped into our heads: "What just hit the windshield?" "Did you see what was growing in that bathroom?" "Kansas doesn't look so flat at night." "If there is a hell, do you think I-70 is it?" We slept in cheap motels because we were too tired to pitch a tent by the time we stopped. We thought we would get farther than we did.

—Lee Bauknight, "Two for the Road"

UNDERSTANDING GRAMMAR

Exercise 21   *SFHB 16a*
Understanding Objects and Complements   *SFW 9a*
                                                       SFC 15a

In the following sentences, underline the boldfaced words once if they are objects and twice if they are subject complements.

1.   Halloween may be the oddest **holiday** of the year.

2.   The roots of Halloween are deeply **religious**.

3.   But Halloween celebrations today seem quite **secular**.

4.   Children and adults wear **costumes** and pull **pranks**.

5.   For all its images of ghosts and goblins, Halloween now seems less **scary**.

In the following sentences, underline the direct objects once and the indirect objects twice.

1. The IRS agent asked the auditor three tough questions.

2. The placement office finds students jobs after college.

3. Did you send Rosa, Peg, Lester, and Davida the same email message?

4. Give Daisy more cookies.

5. The distinguished senator gives proponents of the National Endowment for the Arts headaches.

Underline all the verbal phrases in the following sentences and then indicate whether they function as subjects, objects, complements, adjectives, or adverbs.

1. Waving at the crowd, the winner of the marathon took a victory lap.

2. The waiter certainly seemed eager to please us.

3. The salesperson enjoyed demonstrating the self-closing door on the minivan.

4. Harriet bought an awning to reduce the light streaming through her bay windows.

5. To cherish the weak and the dying was Mother Teresa's mission in life.

6. Reasons to applaud during the candidate's speech were few.

7. Finding an appealing painting at a reasonable price was impossible.

8. The clerk caught Liza sampling the produce.

9. Surprised by the storm front's ferocity, weather forecasters revised their predictions.

10. We decided we finally had sufficient reason to object.

Underline the complete subject once and the complete predicate twice in the following independent clauses. If the subject is understood, write the word understood after the sentence.

1.   The wood on the deck warped after only one summer.

2.   Jeremy has been trying to reach you all day.

3.   Attend the rally this afternoon.

4.   Keeping focused on schoolwork is hard on weekends.

5.   Be careful.

Add an adjective clause to each of the following sentences at the underlines. Remember that adjective clauses are usually introduced by *who, whom, whomever, whose, that,* or *which*. A clause that begins with *where* or *when* is an adjective clause if it modifies a noun.

1. All the students in class who _____ said they supported the Democratic party's proposals.

2. But everyone in the class who _____ opposed the Democrats' policies.

3. Companies that _____ are prospering more today than firms that _____ _____.

4. The original *Star Wars* trilogy, which _____ _____, will soon be joined by a new series of films in the saga.

5. Teens prefer to congregate in places where _____ _____.

6. A person whose _____ is unlikely to find a job quickly.

7. Tom Cruise, who _____, has been an Oscar nominee several times.

8. Tom Cruise, whom _____, remains a top box-office draw.

9. Many youngsters dislike September when _____ _____.

10. The Rolling Stones remain the rock band that _____ _____.

Exercise 26
Understanding Adverb Clauses

SFHB 16d
SFW 9d
SFC 15d

Add an adverb clause to each of the following sentences at the underlines. Remember that adverb clauses are introduced by subordinating conjunctions such as *although, before, since, unless,* and many others.

1.   Even though _____, Americans

      vote in record low numbers.

2.   Many young people put little faith in the social security system

      since _____.

3.   Because _____, many students

      come to college knowing how to operate computers.

4.   If _____, the polar ice caps will

      melt and the level of the oceans will rise.

5.   Although they _____, surprising

      numbers of children still smoke.

Underline all the noun clauses in the following sentences. Then tell whether the clauses are subjects or objects.

1.   What politicians say often matters much less than how they say it.

    _____

2.   Whoever sent a letter of condolence should receive a prompt

    reply from us. _____

3.   Why so many people care so much about celebrities is beyond my

    comprehension. _____

4.   Someone had better explain how the dogs got loose.

    _____

5.   Where you go for a vacation reveals a great deal about who you

    are. _____

Use coordinating conjunctions (*and, or, nor, for, but, yet,* or *so*) to create compound sentences by linking the following pairs of independent clauses.

1.   The stock market finally rose. Investors remained nervous.

2.   Citizens' groups invest time and money on get-out-the-vote campaigns. Many voters still skip general elections.

3.   Vitamin C is good for colds. Vitamin E keeps the skin in good condition.

4.   Most Americans get their news from television. News anchors are powerful people.

5.   Tough drunk-driving laws are fair. There is no reason to tolerate inebriated drivers on the highway.

Create compound sentences by finishing the correlative constructions in each item below. Make sure you have two independent clauses.

1.   If I agree to read *War and Peace* by the end of the summer, then

    you _____.

2.   Either the new owners of the former Soviet Union's nuclear

    weapons will safeguard these deadly stockpiles, or _____

    _____.

3.   Just as eating too much fat contributes to poor physical health, so

    _____.

4.   The First Amendment not only protects speech but also

    _____.

Use a semicolon and the conjunctive adverb in parentheses to link the following pairs of independent clauses. To gain practice punctuating this tricky construction, use the form illustrated in the example—with the semicolon followed immediately by the conjunctive adverb, followed by a comma.

> EXAMPLE   The aircraft lost an engine in flight. It landed safely. (*however*)
>
> REVISED   The aircraft lost an engine in flight; **however,** it landed safely.

1. Ordinary books are still more convenient than most computerized texts. They employ a technology that doesn't go out of date as quickly—paper. (*moreover*)

2. Most people would save money by using public transportation. They elect to use their private automobiles for daily commuting. (*nevertheless*)

3. American colonists resented England's interference in their political and commercial lives. The 13 colonies decided to fight for independence. (*therefore*)

4. German and Japanese automakers discovered that they could build quality products cheaper in North America than at home. Foreign computer manufacturers decided to build silicon-chip plants in the United States. (*similarly*)

5.   Many cities have been unable to meet air-quality standards.

Tougher air-pollution measures have been imposed on their

factories and drivers. (*consequently*)

Build coordinate sentences by combining the following pairs of independent clauses. You may use coordinating conjunctions, correlatives, or conjunctive adverbs. Punctuate with commas, semicolons, or colons.

EXAMPLE	Pencils were invented in the sixteenth century. Erasers were not added until 1858.
REVISED	Pencils were invented in the sixteenth century; **however,** erasers were not added until 1858.

1. Today, French Impressionist paintings are favorites among art lovers. The public loudly rejected them at their debut in the nineteenth century.

2. Painters such as Renoir and Monet wanted art to depict life. They painted common scenes and ordinary people.

3. Many critics of the time were disturbed by the Impressionists' banal subjects. They thought the Impressionists' paintings themselves looked crude and unfinished.

4. The official Salon refused to hang the Impressionists' works. The painters were forced to exhibit independently.

5. The Impressionists refused to abandon their examination of modern life. They refused to change their style to please the critics.

Use semicolons, colons, or dashes to link the following pairs of independent clauses.

1.   Don't feel sorry for the spare and thorny plants you see in a desert. They don't want or need more water.

2.   Barren stalks, wicked thorns, and waxy spines are their adaptations to a harsh environment. Such features conserve water or protect the plants from desert animals and birds.

3.   Spring rains can create an astonishing desert spectacle. Cacti and other plants explode into colorful bloom.

4.   Even the dour prickly pear bears handsome flowers. You've got to see the display to believe it.

5.   Many animals call the desert home too, from tiny lizards to scrawny coyotes. They are just as well adapted as the plants.

Join the following pairs of sentences by changing one independent clause of each pair into a subordinate clause.

1. The original books of Babylonia and Assyria were collections of inscribed clay tablets stored in labeled containers too heavy for one person to move. We think of books as portable, bound volumes.

2. Clay tablets had many drawbacks. They remained the most convenient medium for recording information until the Egyptians developed papyrus around 3000 BC.

3. Egyptian books were lighter than clay tablets but still awkward to carry or read. A single papyrus book comprised several large, unwieldy scrolls.

4. The Greeks developed papyrus leaflets. They folded and bound the leaflets to produce the first modern-looking book.

5. That first book was the Greek Bible. It takes its name from Byblos, the Phoenician city that supplied Greece with papyrus.

Rewrite the following sentences to reduce any undue complexity in subordination and in other modification. If necessary, break longer sentences into shorter ones.

1.   Although for many years scientists believed that there might be another planet on the fringes of the solar system whose gravitational pull influenced the orbit of Uranus, there was no concrete evidence that this additional planet existed, even though astronomers spent decades speculating about its mass, distance from Earth, and orbital mechanics.

2.   Because the orbit of Uranus seemed oddly influenced by an unseen planetary body, scientists searched for other objects until they actually discovered Neptune and, later, Pluto, which, unfortunately, did not seem to have the mass necessary to explain the orbital disruptions of Uranus that prompted the explorations.

3.   If a mysterious Planet X at the fringes of the solar system is an appealing notion, few scientists now take the idea seriously because *Voyager 2* provided data that suggested that the mass of Uranus is exactly what it should be if we calculate its orbit accurately.

4.   Some scientists now are debating whether Pluto itself is a real planet because rather than resembling other planets it is more like a group of asteroid-like bodies at the fringe of the solar system, which are much smaller than planets, which have irregular shapes, and which do not have atmospheres.

Revise the following sentences to avoid inconsistent patterns or faulty parallel structures.

1. On opening night at the new Tex-Mex restaurant, the manager called the servers together to be sure they understood all the items on the menu, could pronounce *fajitas*, and that they would remember to ask "Salt or no salt?" when customers ordered margaritas.

2. Two servers had a wager to see whose customers would order the most drinks, devour the most chips, and, of course, the biggest gratuities.

3. Offering the best Southwestern cuisine and to serve the hottest salsa were the restaurant's two goals.

4. But customers soon made it clear that they also expected real barbecue on the menu, so the manager added slow-cooked beef ribs smothered in sauce, hefty racks of pork ribs dripping with fat, and there was smoked sausage on the menu too that was juicy and hot.

5. Servers had to explain to tourists that one was supposed to eat beef ribs with one's fingers, wrap one's own fajitas, and to bite into jalapeños very carefully.

Rewrite the following sentences to eliminate any sentence fragments.

1.   Although most movie stars are human and were created by the usual birds-and-bees process. One of the most popular movie stars ever, the liquid metal cyborg in *Terminator 2*, was created by a computer.

2.   The technology of computer animation has developed rapidly over the past decade. Making a spectacular range of special effects possible.

3.   Industrial Light and Magic was responsible for the astonishing cyborg. A special-effects company owned by director George Lucas.

4.   The company was founded to create the special effects for *Star Wars*. Subsequently creating the special effects for a string of hits, including *E.T.: The Extra-Terrestrial* and *Who Framed Roger Rabbit?* Also the special effects for *Ghost*.

5.   While the cyborg appears in *Terminator 2* for only about five minutes, creating the footage cost millions of dollars. Keeping thirty-five computer animators busy for ten months.

Exercise 37
Understanding Intentional Fragments

SFHB 35b
SFW 31b
SFC 30b

Bring to class some advertisements that use intentional fragments or locate a Web site or listserv that routinely includes fragments. Working with other students in a small group, identify these fragments; then join forces to rewrite them and eliminate all incomplete sentences. Assess the difference between the originals and the revised versions. Why do you think the writers used fragments?

Correct the comma splices in the following sentences.

1. At one time the walls in many Philadelphia neighborhoods were covered with graffiti, however, they are covered with murals today.

2. Since 1984 a city-sponsored program has been teaming young graffiti writers with professional artists, the result is the creation of over a thousand works of public art.

3. The murals are large, they are colorful, they are 99 percent graffiti-free.

4. A forty-foot-tall mural of Julius ("Dr. J") Erving has become a local landmark, even Dr. J himself brings friends by to see it.

5. The theory behind the program is that graffiti writers, being inherently artistic, will not deface a work of art they respect, so far the theory holds.

Revise these sentences to eliminate run-on sentences.

1. Centuries of superstition and ignorance have given bats a bad reputation millions of the flying mammals are killed each year in a misguided effort to protect livestock, crops, and people.

2. Entire species of bats are being wiped out at an alarming rate for example in the 1960s a new species of fruit-eating bat was discovered in the Philippines by the 1980s it was extinct.

3. In truth, bats are industrious and invaluable members of the natural order they spread the seeds of hundreds of species of plants.

4. Strange as it may sound, bats are essential to the economies of many countries the plants they pollinate or seed include such cash crops as bananas, figs, dates, vanilla beans, and avocados.

5. Many plants essential to such delicate ecosystems as the African savanna and the South American rain forest rely solely on bats for propagating should the bats disappear the entire system could collapse.

Rewrite or rearrange these sentences, placing modifiers in appropriate positions. You may need to add a noun for the modifier to modify. Not all of the sentences need to be revised.

1. Although among the most famous of reptiles, biologists have only recently begun to study rattlesnakes.

2. The deadly snakes, which take their name from the two characteristic pits on their snouts, belong to the family of pit vipers.

3. After studying the habits of pit vipers, the pits, which serve as infrared sensors and enable the snakes to seek heat, evolved to detect danger rather than to hunt prey.

4. Given their lethal capabilities, it is not surprising that pit vipers are universally loathed.

5. Despite their fearful reputation, however, people are seldom bitten unless the snakes are provoked.

Rewrite each of the following sentences so that each adjective in parentheses modifies an appropriate noun or pronoun. Place the adjectives before or after the words they modify, and punctuate them correctly.

1.   The elm trees once common throughout North America have disappeared, victims of disease. (*towering; graceful; Dutch-elm*)

2.   This infection destroys the vascular system of the elm, causing trees to become husks in a few short weeks. (*fungal; relentless; mature; thriving; leafless*)

3.   Few parks in the United States can match the diversity of New York's Central Park, with its zoo, gardens and fields, ponds and lakes, and museums. (*great urban; sizable; pleasant; glistening; world class*)

4.   The city seems to stop at the edge of the park where New Yorkers can stroll quietly under a canopy of shade trees or strap on roller blades and buzz tourists. (*noisy; crowded; sprawling; business-suited or casual; cool; green; curious; delighted*)

5.   Bankers, show people, and street people alike jostle shoulders and shopping bags in this oasis. (*wealthy; glittering; down-on-their-luck; refreshing; urban*)

Rearrange adjectives to make each of these sentences clearer or more effective. Several options are possible.

1.   Lisa and Julia wanted to find a women's group that could help them plan their strategy for lobbying and that was politically sophisticated.

2.   Professional children's care in the workplace of employed parents was one of their goals.

3.   They viewed the negative board members' attitudes to their persuasive abilities as a challenge.

4.   Before explaining their plan, Lisa asked for the undivided employees' attention.

5.   Obtaining an endorsement was essential if they were to overcome the stubborn management's resistance.

In these sentences, replace each boldfaced modifier with a better one.

1. In the United States, most people feel **confidently** that their

    drinking water is safe.

2. In many parts of the world, however, even water that looks **well**

    can be full of bacteria and pollution.

3. Some major relief organizations, such as the International Rescue

    Committee, feel **optimistically** that they can bring clean water to

    the rural areas of Africa and India.

4. They teach villagers what must be done to keep a sanitation

    system running **good**.

5. Parents who know that their children's drinking water should be

    boiled feel **badly** because often they cannot afford the fuel to boil

    it.

Working with other students in a group, read over these sentences and decide which ones have faulty modifiers. Confer to decide how any problems with modifiers might be solved.

1. Ms. Oliveras was disappointed with the grant proposals she read—she thought the projects they proposed should have been more unique.

2. She was looking for a very singular plan in which to invest the foundation's money.

3. The board of trustees had most definite opinions about what constituted "community values," a situation that made her a little nervous.

4. But because her knowledge of the community was less complete than theirs, she felt she better understood what was important.

5. When she finally came across the B'nai B'rith proposal for a preschool learning center, she decided it was the most perfect one for meeting the needs of the town.

Rewrite each of the following sentences so that each adverb in parentheses modifies an appropriate verb, adjective, or adverb. Notice which adverbs work best in one position only and which can be moved more freely in a sentence.

1. The elm trees once common throughout North America have disappeared, victims of disease. (*sadly; quite; almost; completely*)

2. This lethal infection destroys the vascular system of the elm, causing trees to become husks in a few short weeks. (*nearly; always; completely*)

3. The delicate paintings had not been packed, so they arrived damaged. (*extremely; well; severely*)

4. Annoyed, the senator replied to the reporter in an angry tone. (*visibly; unusually*)

5. We left the photo shop poorer but better equipped for difficult telephoto shots. (*considerably; much; extremely*)

Rewrite the sentences so that every adverb clearly modifies the intended word.

1.   People who attend the theater regularly complain that the manners of the average audience member are in severe decline.

2.   Far from listening in respectful if not attentive silence, he broadcasts a running commentary frequently modeled, no doubt, on his behavior in front of the television at home.

3.   Sitting next to a woman who spends most of the evening unwrapping cellophane-covered candies slowly can provoke even the most saintly theatergoer to violence.

4.   Cellular phones, beepers, and wristwatch alarms even go off intermittently causing an evening in the theater to resemble a trip to an electronics store.

5.   For their part, actors marvel at how audiences today only manage to cough during the quietest moments of a play.

Exercise 47
Avoiding Double Negatives

Eliminate double negatives by rewriting sentences that contain them. Not every sentence is faulty.

1. Some critics claim that in this age of videos, computers, and the Internet, young people don't hardly read anymore.

2. Yet cities like Madison, Wisconsin, which are centers of education and technology, haven't never had so many bookstores.

3. Many bookstores aren't no longer just places to buy books.

4. They serve as community centers where people can buy coffee, go to poetry seminars, and get on the Internet without never buying any books.

5. But bookstore owners know that scarcely any browsers leave the store empty-handed.

For each sentence, underline the appropriate form in parentheses.

1.   Today community librarians are constantly trying to decide what is (*more, most*) important: expanding computer facilities or buying more books.

2.   These librarians consider who among their clients has the (*greater, greatest*) need—school children, working adults, or retired people.

3.   In general, librarians enjoy the reputation of being among the (*most helpful, helpfullest*) of city employees.

4.   In good libraries, librarians are also likely to be among the (*most bright, brightest*) city employees.

5.   Well-trained librarians, or information specialists as they are often called today, will find their (*better, best*) job prospects in medium-sized cities with a growing population.

Exercise 49   *SFHB 22a*
Making Verbs Agree with Their Subjects   *SFW 33a*
                                                                 SFC 17a

For each sentence, underline the correct verb in parentheses.

1.   Storms of all types (*continue, continues*) to intrigue people.

2.   The storm chaser, like other thrill seekers, (*learn, learns*) to
        minimize the dangers of the hunt.

3.   It's unlikely that either the dangers or the boredom of storm
        chasing (*is, are*) going to discourage the dedicated amateur.

4.   The meteorologist and storm chaser (*know, knows*) that neither
        ferocious tornadoes nor the less violent waterspout (*is, are*)
        predictable.

5.   That the last ten years have seen an increase in the numbers of
        storm chasers (*is, are*) certain.

Making Verbs Agree with Indefinite Pronoun Subjects *SFW 33b*
                                                         SFC 17b

For each sentence, underline the verb that would be correct for academic writing.

1.   Most of New York's immigrants (*is, are*) now non-European.

2.   Everybody (*seem, seems*) to have something to contribute.

3.   Nobody in the city (*run, runs*) politics anymore.

4.   Everybody (*expect, expects*) a piece of the pie.

5.   None of the candidates (*is, are*) qualified.

6.   All of the groups in the city (*want, wants*) to be heard.

Decide whether the collective subjects in the following sentences are being treated as singular or plural. Then underline the verb that is correct for academic writing.

1. Lieutenant Data (*reports, report*) to Captain Picard that the data on Klingon encroachments of the neutral zone (*is, are*) not subject to interpretation.

2. The crew of the Federation starship (*is, are*) eager to resolve the conflict.

3. Five years (*has, have*) passed since the last intergalactic crisis.

4. A number of weapons still (*needs, need*) to be brought online, but the chief engineer reports that the actual number of inoperative systems (*is, are*) small.

5. The jury (*is, are*) still out as to whether a committee of Federation officials (*intends, intend*) to authorize action against the Klingons.

For each sentence, choose the correct verb for academic writing.

1.   As the end of the twentieth century begins, most politicians,
      regardless of their party or ideology, *(embrace, embraces)* the
      idea that every child should be able to read by the end of third
      grade.

2.   Almost everyone *(agree, agrees)* with this laudable goal, but
      trained educators who understand the complex process of
      learning to read are suspicious of this bandwagon approach.

3.   Children's ability to learn how to read *(depend, depends)* on a
      combination of psychological, physical, and social factors.

4.   Moreover, many children from families in low-income
      neighborhoods, all too common in major cities today, *(need,
      needs)* intensive tutoring because they are not ready to learn when
      they arrive in kindergarten.

5.   The HOSTS tutoring program, which has had great success in
      helping children to start reading, *(require, requires)* as many as
      fifty volunteers in a small elementary school, and such volunteers
      can be hard to find.

For each sentence, underline the correct verb.

1.   The mayor of the town (*strides, stride*) to the microphone.

2.   Among the grumbles from the reporters, the crowd (*take, takes*) their seats.

3.   (*Does, Do*) the mayor's decision to fire Carey surprise anyone after the last election?

4.   The city council president claims that she is one of those people who (*objects, object*) most strongly to politics taking precedence over community unity.

5.   But she knows she's not the only one who (*wants, want*) a nationally admired park system.

Fill in each blank with the verb and tense indicated in parentheses. Use active voice unless passive is specified.

1.   In Shakespeare's tragedy *Macbeth*, three witches tell Macbeth that

        someday he _____ Scotland. (*rule*—future)

2.   Macbeth quickly explains to his wife, the ambitious Lady

        Macbeth, what the witches _____ him earlier that

        day: the Scottish crown. (*promise*—past perfect)

3.   Lady Macbeth, even more ambitious than her husband,

        immediately _____ a plot to murder King Duncan

        that very night and then _____ her husband to do

        the horrid deed. (*devise*—present; *convince*—present)

4.   But even though the plot succeeds and Macbeth becomes king,

        the new ruler fears that he _____ by other

        ambitious men. (*challenge*—future, passive voice)

5.   Macbeth is finally slain by Macduff, whose wife and children

        _____ earlier in the play at Macbeth's orders.

        (*slaughter*—past perfect, passive voice)

For each sentence, underline the correct verb form from the choices in parentheses.

1. Alex wondered whether the mayor had (*spoke, spoken*) too soon in welcoming everyone to participate in the town meeting.

2. The residents of Oakhill had not (*took, taken*) much interest in the environmental issue until this meeting.

3. Now the Oakhill representative pulled a petition out of her purse and (*sat, set*) it before the mayor.

4. She claimed that she had (*got, gotten*) more than enough signatures to stop the proposed freeway extension.

5. Alex had to admit that Oakhill had (*chose, chosen*) well, for the representative was an effective activist.

Underline the passive verbs in the following sentences and then revise those passive verbs that might be better stated in the active voice. Some sentences may require no revision.

1.   Even opponents of chemical pesticides sometimes use poisons after they have been bitten by fire ants, aggressive and vicious insects spreading throughout the southern United States.

2.   These tiny creatures have been given by nature a fierce sting, and they usually attack en masse.

3.   Gardeners are hampered in their work by the mounds erected by the ants.

4.   By the time a careless gardener discovers a mound, a hand or foot has likely been bitten by numerous ants.

5.   The injured appendage feels as if it has been attacked by a swarm of bees.

In the following sentences, underline verbs in the subjunctive mood.

1.   It is essential that we be at the airport at 2:00 p.m. today.

2.   I wish I were less susceptible to telephone solicitors!

3.   Far be it from me to criticize your writing!

4.   Come what may, the show must go on.

5.   If Avery were to arrive early, what would happen to our plans?

6.   It is essential that you take over as the supervisor.

Revise or rewrite the following sentences to eliminate vague pronouns. Treat the sentences as a continuous passage.

1.   Leah read avidly about gardening, although she had never planted

       one herself.

2.   Her fondness for the convenience of apartment living left Leah

       without a place for one.

3.   Leah found herself buying garden tools, seeds, and catalogs, but

       it did not make much sense.

4.   Leah's friends suggested that she build planters on her deck or

       install a garden window, but Leah doubted that the landlord

       would permit it.

5.   As for her parents' idea that she invest in a condominium, they

       overestimated her bank account.

Revise the following sentences to eliminate ambiguous pronoun references. Treat the sentences as a continuous passage. Several versions of each sentence may be possible.

1. Amanda could hardly believe that the representatives from Habitat for Humanity would visit Madison, Wisconsin, when it was so bad.

2. When she met them at their hotel, the winds were howling, the visitors were hungry, and it was getting worse.

3. But the two women were bundled up and ready to brave the elements, so she figured this wasn't a problem.

4. Later Amanda learned that one of the visitors, Sarah Severson, had been born in Wisconsin, and she told her she knew a great deal about northern winters.

5. The three of them took off through the snow in Amanda's lumbering SUV, but it didn't slow them down a bit.

Underline the boldfaced pronouns that you think a reader might find unclear. Revise the sentences as necessary.

1. Even tourists just visiting the building soon noticed the aging state capitol's sagging floors, unreliable plumbing, and exposed electrical conduits. **This** was embarrassing.

2. When an electrical fire in the office of the Speaker of the House was followed soon by another in the Senate chamber, it was clear **it** was a problem.

3. Old paintings and sculptures were grimy and cracked, **which** had been donated by citizens over the decades.

4. The governor proposed reconstructing the state capitol, **which** the legislators endorsed almost unanimously.

5. **This** was passed by a voice vote.

Revise the following sentences wherever pronouns and antecedents do not agree in number. You may change either the pronouns or the antecedents.

1. Many a college class is conducted using the Socratic method, but they aren't always successful.

2. In the Socratic method, a teacher leads a student through a series of questions to conclusions that they believe they've reached without the instructor's prompting.

3. Yet when instructors ask leading questions, the cleverer students sometimes answer it in unexpected ways.

4. However, no instructor, except perhaps for Socrates himself, could foresee all the questions and answers eager students might have for them.

5. But an instructor can be as open as students to accepting new ideas when lively debates lead them to question their beliefs.

Exercise 62
Making Pronouns Agree with Collective Antecedents

SFHB 27c
SFW 35b
SFC 22c

In the following sentences, underline the appropriate word in parentheses. Antecedents are in boldface type.

1.   The **class** entered the lecture hall and took (*its, their*) seats, eager to hear from the architect after (*its, their*) field trip to several of his buildings.

2.   He belonged to a revitalized **school** of design that had enjoyed (*its, their*) best days four decades ago.

3.   The aging architect was accompanied by several **members** of his firm, carrying (*its, their*) designs in huge portfolios.

4.   Students hoped that the **board of directors** of the college might give (*its, their*) blessing to a commission by the architect.

5.   Any **panel** of experts was likely to cast (*its, their*) vote in favor of such a project.

Underline the italicized word or phrase that would be correct in formal and college writing.

1. Anybody can learn to drive an automobile with a manual transmission if (*they are, he or she is*) coordinated.

2. But not everyone will risk (*his or her life, their lives*) trying.

3. Few today seem eager to take (*his or her, their*) driver's tests in a five-speed.

4. Everyone learning to drive a manual car expects (*his or her, their*) car to stall at the most inopportune moment.

5. Most of all, nobody wants to stop (*his or her, their*) manual-shift car on a steep hill.

Exercise 64
Using Pronouns with Two Antecedents

SFHB 27d
SFW 35b
SFC 22d

In these sentences, underline the appropriate italicized words.

1.	Neither the tour guide nor his customers had bothered to confirm (*his, their*) flight from Chicago's O'Hare Airport back to Toledo.

2.	Either the ticket agents or a woman working the check-in desk had misread (*their, her*) computer terminal and accidentally canceled the group's reservations.

3.	Either the tourists or their guide had to make up (*their minds, his mind*) quickly about arranging transportation back to Toledo.

4.	Neither the guide nor his wife relished the thought of spending (*his, her, their*) hard-earned money on yet another expensive ticket.

5.	Wandering about the vast terminal, the guide located a commuter airline willing to fly either the group or its bags to (*its, their*) destination cheaply.

Underline the correct pronouns from the choices offered in parentheses.

1.   In the reporter's opinion, neither (*she, her*) nor her competitors
      had done a good job in covering the city's financial crisis.

2.   It was likely that both political parties would now accuse (*she,
      her*) and (*they, them*) of media bias.

3.   Knowing her colleagues at the competing TV stations, the
      reporter was convinced that both she and (*they, them*) had rushed
      their stories.

4.   She had assumed that the city manager's staff had been honest
      about the financial problems, but now she wasn't sure they had
      been truthful with (*she, her*).

5.   "You and (*I, me*) will just have to accept the criticism," the
      reporter told a professional colleague, who just frowned at (*she,
      her*).

Underline the correct italicized pronouns.

1. Sam Donaldson looks like a man (*whom, who*) wouldn't trust a nun with a prayer.

2. (*Whom, Who*) wouldn't like to win the state lottery?

3. To (*who, whom*) would you go for sound financial advice?

4. Are these the children (*who, whom*) you took by bus to Santa Fe?

5. Officials couldn't determine (*who, whom*) rigged the beauty contest.

Exercise 67
Choosing Pronoun Case in Comparisons

SFHB 28a
SFW 35c
SFC 23a

Underline the correct italicized pronouns.

1. Although the Cowardly Lion needed the Wizard's help as much as Dorothy did, the King of the Jungle was less determined than (*she, her*) to hike to Oz.

2. Dorothy probably felt more confident than (*he, him*) that she could deal with the wonderful Wizard.

3. Perhaps Dorothy could relate more easily to (*he, him*) than a lion could.

4. Although more cautious in his appraisal of the Wizard than Dorothy, the Scarecrow was no less eager for guidance than (*she, her*).

5. Perhaps the Scarecrow even feared that Dorothy would like the Wizard more than (*he, him*).

Underline the correct italicized pronouns.

1. That is (*he, him*) in the office there.

2. The guilty party certainly was not (*she, her*).

3. Spying three men in uniform, we assumed that the pilots were (*they, them*).

4. They are (*who, whom*)?

5. We were surprised that the person who had complained was (*she, her*).

Underline all occurrences of *its/it's* in the following sentences and correct any errors by writing the correct form in the space of above the error.

1. Its been decades since Americans have felt as comfortable

    traveling in Eastern Europe as they do now.

2. Its likely that tourism will soon become a major industry in

    Hungary, Poland, and the Czech Republic.

3. Each of these countries has much to attract tourists to its cities.

4. Yet its the small towns of Eastern Europe that many Americans

    may find most appealing.

5. In rural areas, sensitive travelers often get a better feel for a

    country and its people.

Underline and correct any pronoun-related errors in the sentences below.

1. There is usually not much doubt about whose responsible for

    enormous environmental disasters.

2. Its not hard to spot a capsized oil tanker.

3. Yet you're home or yard can contribute to environmental

    pollution.

4. The earth is our's to protect or despoil.

5. Ecology has to be everyone's responsibility.

Underline the correct italicized pronouns.

1. Charlie Chaplin's tramp—(*that, which, who*) wore a derby, baggy

    trousers, and a mustache—may still be the most recognized

    character on film.

2. The popularity (*that, which, who*) Chaplin had in the early days

    of film may never be equaled either.

3. His graceful gestures and matchless acrobatics, (*that, which, who*)

    some critics likened to ballet, were perfectly suited to the silent

    screen.

4. A flaw (*that, which, who*) weakens many of Chaplin's films is

    sentimentality.

5. Chaplin's tramp made a last appearance in *The Great Dictator*

    (1940), (*that, which, who*) satirized Hitler's regime.

Underline the correct tense—simple present or present progressive.

1. Many people have bizarre dreams, but I usually (*dream, am dreaming*) about something that (*happens, is happening*) during the day.

2. I often (*remember, am remembering*) my dreams right after I (*wake, am waking*) up.

3. Sometimes if I (*hear, am hearing*) a noise while I (*dream, am dreaming*), I will incorporate that into my dream.

4. I (*know, am knowing*) a lot about dreams because I (*write, am writing*) a paper about them this semester.

5. To prepare for the paper, I (*research, am researching*) many psychological explanations for various dream symbols, such as snakes, bodies of water, and people.

6. I'm not sure if I (*believe, am believing*) those explanations, but they are very interesting.

Underline the best verb tense—simple past or present perfect. Use the present perfect whenever possible.

1. This month, the newspapers (*had, have had*) many articles about a phenomenon called the glass ceiling.

2. This term refers to an unofficial limitation on promotion for women who (*worked, have worked*) in a corporation for several years and who cannot advance beyond middle management.

3. Last year my mother (*applied, has applied*) for the position of vice president of the company she works for, but the company (*did not promote, have not promoted*) her.

4. She (*had, has had*) the most experience of all the candidates for the job, but a man was chosen instead.

5. She (*was, has been*) with that company for ten years. Now she doesn't know how much longer she will stay there.

Fill in the blanks with the most precise and appropriate tense of the verb talk. Pay special attention to time words. For numbers 3 and 10, incorporate the adverbs in parentheses into your answers.

1. The employees _____ about the issue since yesterday.

2. Some employees _____ about it when we arrived at work.

3. They _____ about the issue when they leave work. (*probably*)

4. We _____ about it many times in the past.

5. I never _____ about this topic last week.

6. We _____ about this problem for two hours by the time the president visited our office.

7. Workers _____ about this issue quite often these days.

8. They _____ about the subject right now.

9. After they _____ about it for many weeks, they reached a consensus.

10. They _____ about this issue again. (*never*)

Exercise 75
ESL Correcting English Verbs

SFHB 32a,b,c
SFW 36a
SFC 27a,b,c

Each of the following sentences contains errors related to verb tense, transitive/intransitive verbs, and two-word verbs. Underline the errors and correct them.

1. Before I study psychology, I thought it was an easy subject.

2. Now I am knowing that it isn't easy.

3. It has had a lot of statistics.

4. I am studying psychology since April, and I only begin to learn some of the concepts.

5. I have been tried to learn more of the concepts every day.

6. Last night, I have studied from 9:00 to midnight.

7. I went my adviser last Monday.

8. She told to me to see her after class.

9. But when I went to see her after class, she already left.

10. It's January. By the middle of June, I have studied psychology for six months.

Fill in the blanks with an appropriate modal from the list below. More than one answer is possible for each blank. Try not to use each modal more than once.

would	must	have to	ought to
should have	should	can	might
had better	must have		

1. Can you believe the line waiting to see the movie *Spider-man*?

   That _____ be a good movie!

2. Where is my purse, Mom? It _____ be on the

   table where you put it last night.

3. I'm sorry, Professor Lopez, but I _____ not

   take the test tomorrow because I _____ go to

   Immigration about my visa.

4. Jason, you _____ eat your vegetables or you

   won't get any dessert.

Each of the following sentences contains errors related to modal auxiliaries. Underline the errors and correct them.

1. Megan's boss told her, "You had better to improve your attitude, or we will have to take disciplinary action."

2. Megan was very distressed by this news; she did not could understand the basis for her boss's complaints.

3. She tried to think of things that she had done wrong. She knew that she should had been more enthusiastic at the last meeting, but she felt she couldn't be hypocritical. She simply didn't agree with her boss.

4. Megan was really worried. Her boss mights send her a "pink slip," which would mean that she had been fired.

Exercise 78
ESL Distinguishing between Count and
Noncount Nouns

SFHB 33b
SFW 36d
SFC 28b

Below is a list of nouns. Write *C* after the count nouns and *NC* after the noncount nouns. If you are not sure, consult an ESL dictionary. Then make a note of the nouns you had to check.

1.	furniture	_____	2.	work	_____
3.	dollar	_____	4.	job	_____
5.	advice	_____	6.	people	_____
7.	equipment	_____	8.	money	_____
9.	newspaper	_____	10.	traffic	_____

Each of the following sentences has at least one error in articles or quantifiers. Underline each error and correct it.

1.   Much people have visited the new restaurant downtown called

Rock-and-Roll Hamburger Haven.

2.   Most of customers are young people because music in restaurant

is very loud.

3.   The restaurant serves the usual food—hamburgers, pizza, and

pasta. It is not expensive; in fact, most expensive item on the

menu is only $8.

4.   Food is not very good, but the atmosphere is very appealing to

these young men and women.

5.   There are much posters on the walls of famous rock star. There is

even authentic motorcycle of one star.

6.   Some of regular customers say they have seen some stars eating

there.

7.   These "regulars" give these advices to anyone who wants to spot

a star there—look for dark glasses and a leather coat.

UNDERSTANDING PUNCTUATION AND MECHANICS

Exercise 80
Using End Punctuation

SFHB 34
SFW 37
SFC 29

Edit the following passage, adding, replacing, and deleting periods, question marks, exclamation points, and any other marks of punctuation that need to be changed.

1. Hannibal simply outfoxed the Roman general Varro at Cannae!!!

2. Hannibal placed his numerically smaller army where the Aufidius River would protect his flank—could the hotheaded Varro appreciate such a move—and arrayed his forces to make the Roman numbers work against themselves!

3. It must have seemed obvious to Hannibal where Varro would concentrate his forces?

4. "Advance!," Hannibal ordered!

5. Is it likely that Varro and the Romans noticed how thin the Carthaginian forces were at the center of the battle line?

6. Predictably, the Romans pressed their attack on the weakened Carthaginian center. But in the meantime, Hannibal's cavalry had destroyed its Roman counterpart!

7. You might be wondering, "Why didn't Hannibal use his cavalry to strengthen his weak center"?

8. It was because he wanted it behind the Roman lines to attack

    from the rear!

9. Hannibal expected the troops at the ends of his battle line to

    outflank the Romans, but would such a strategy work.

10. It did! The Romans found themselves surrounded and defeated!

Insert commas where needed in these sentences.

1. When Mount Saint Helens erupted in 1980 the north slope collapsed sending torrents of mud and rock down into the Toutle River valley.

2. Stripped of all vegetation for fifteen miles the valley was left virtually lifeless; whatever trees there were were dead.

3. In an effort to prevent erosion and speed the valley's recovery ecologists planted grasses and ground covers.

4. However the species they planted were not native but alien or exotic.

5. All things considered the scientists probably should have left nature to take its course since the alien plants are now inhibiting the regrowth of native species.

Exercise 82
Using Commas to Enclose Sentence Elements

Decide which modifiers are nonessential in the following sentences and enclose them in commas.

1. Carter a sales clerk with a passion for Native American art urged Iona his manager at a gallery in Alpine to increase her stock of Navajo rugs.

2. On a sales trip, Carter had met with several art dealers who specialized in Native American crafts; the dealer whom Carter met in Tuba City had offered rugs produced by several well-known artists.

3. The rugs that he showed Carter included examples of all the classic Navajo designs produced from wool which the weavers had shorn, carded, and dyed themselves.

4. Iona who had managed the store for ten years was uncertain that her regular customers would buy the premium rugs which cost as much as $6,000.

5. But because Iona the lover of art was more speculative than Iona the businesswoman, the gallery soon featured a selection of Navajo rugs which quickly increased sales.

Add commas to the following sentences if they are needed to link ideas, and move commas that are misplaced. Some sentences may be correct.

1. As the mower cut its final swath across the deep green grass, the long golden rays of the setting sun toyed listlessly with the dancing grasshoppers in its wake.

2. Although all of the day's daylilies had already closed up shop the night-blooming flowers were starting to offer their perfumes to the hushed expectant air.

3. An orchestra of crickets tree frogs and, whippoorwills warmed up for the evening's concert; fireflies silently urgently signaled their ardor in the undergrowth.

4. Overhead, the moon's bright silver slipper held court with an audience of stars: Orion the Pleiades Pegasus Cassiopeia.

5. Wafting romantically out of the gazebo and across the lawn, Heather slipped on a lone red roller skate and pitched headlong into the pool.

Exercise 84
Omitting Unnecessary Commas

SFHB 36d
SFW 38d
SFC 31d

Draw a slash through all commas that cause awkward interruptions in the following sentences.

1. Psychologists, who have studied moods, say that such emotional states are contagious, and compare them to social viruses.

2. Moreover, some people are emotionally expressive, and likely to transmit moods; others, seem to be more inclined to "catch" moods.

3. Trying to pinpoint the exact means by which moods are transmitted, is difficult, since the process happens almost instantaneously.

4. One transmission mechanism is imitation: by unconsciously imitating facial expressions, people produce in themselves a mood, that goes with the expression.

5. Generally, people who get along well with others, synchronize their moods, by making a series of changes in their body language.

87

Add commas where necessary to the following sentences.

1.   In the autumn of 1863, Abraham Lincoln President of the United
     States traveled to Gettysburg Pennsylvania to speak at the
     dedication of a cemetery there.

2.   The cemetery was for the soldiers who had fallen at the Battle of
     Gettysburg, and Lincoln's speech—now known as the Gettysburg
     Address—opened with the famous words "Fourscore and seven
     years ago."

3.   The Battle of Gettysburg had started on July 1 1863 and had
     raged for three days.

4.   The Civil War would not end until April 1865.

5.   The bloodiest battle of the war took place near Sharpsburg
     Maryland along the banks of Antietam Creek where a single day
     of fighting produced over 23000 casualties.

Revise the following sentences, adding or deleting semicolons for correct usage. Not all the semicolons are incorrect. You may have to substitute other punctuation marks for some of the semicolons.

1. For many years, biblical spectacles were a staple of the Hollywood film industry, however, in recent years few such films have been produced.

2. Cecil B. DeMille made the grandest epics; he is quoted as saying; "Give me any couple of pages of the Bible and I'll give you a picture."

3. He made *The Ten Commandments* twice, the 1956 version starred Charlton Heston as Moses.

4. The most famous scene in *The Ten Commandments* is the parting of the Red Sea; the waters opening to enable the Israelites to escape the pursuing army of Pharaoh.

5. DeMille made many nonbiblical movies, some of them, however, were also epic productions with casts of thousands and spectacular settings.

Use each of the following groups of clauses, phrases, and bits of information to make a single sentence, using semicolons as necessary. You may have to add some words and ideas.

1. The action in mad-killer movies like *Scream*. A masked killer dispatches random teenagers and even an occasional high school principal. A masked killer attacks the annoying reporter, Gale Weathers. A masked killer attacks and, maybe, kills Dewey, the bumbling cop.

2. Strange titles of Bob Dylan songs from the 1960s. "Subterranean Homesick Blues" "It's Alright, Ma (I'm Only Bleeding)" "Love Minus Zero/No Limit" " Don't Think Twice, It's All Right" "I Shall Be Free—No. 10."

3. Items in E. D. Hirsch's list of everything Americans should know. Carbon-14 dating. "*Veni, vidi, vici.*" "Doctor Livingstone, I presume." "Yes, Virginia, there is a Santa Claus."

4. Exceptionally long movie titles. *Alice Doesn't Live Here Anymore. They Shoot Horses, Don't They? Jo Jo Dancer, Your Life Is Calling. The Effect of Gamma Rays on Man-in-the-Moon Marigolds. Close Encounters of the Third Kind: The Special Edition.*

Revise the following sentences by adding colons where they are needed or deleting them if they are used incorrectly. Don't assume that every sentence contains an error.

1.   No one ever forgets the conclusion of Hitchcock's *Psycho*; the discovery of Norman's mother in the rocking chair.

2.   Hitchcock liked to use memorable settings in his films, including: Mt. Rushmore in *North by Northwest*, Radio City Music Hall in *Saboteur*, and the British Museum in *Blackmail*.

3.   One actor appears in every Hitchcock film Hitchcock himself.

4.   *Rear Window* is a cinematic tour de force: all the action focuses on what Jimmy Stewart sees from his window.

5.   Hitchcock probably summed up his own technique best; "There is no terror in a bang, only in the anticipation of it."

Rework the following passage by adding or deleting quotation marks, moving punctuation as necessary, and marking paragraphs for indention (¶) where you think appropriate.

Much to the tourists' surprise, their "uproar" over conditions at their so-called "luxury resort" attracted the attention of a local television station. (In fact, Mrs. Rattle had read "the riot act" to a consumer advocate who worked for the station.) A reporter interviewed Mrs. Rattle, who claimed that she had been promised luxury accommodations. This place smells like old fish, she fumed. Even the roaches look unwell. Didn't you check out the accommodations before paying? the reporter asked, turning to Mr. Rattle. He replied that unfortunately they had prepaid the entire vacation. But Mrs. Rattle interrupted. I knew we should have gone to Paris. You never said that! Mr. Rattle objected. As I was trying to say, Mrs. Rattle continued, I'd even rather be in Philadelphia.

Abridge the following passage, using at least three ellipses. Draw a line through the parts you want to omit and place the ellipsis dots in the space above the omission. Be sure the passage is still readable after you have made your cuts.

Within a week, the neglected Victorian-style house being repaired by volunteers began to look livable again, its gables repaired, its gutters rehung, its roof reshingled. Even the grand staircase, rickety and worm-eaten, had been rebuilt. The amateur artisans made numerous mistakes during the project, including painting several windows shut, papering over a heating register, and hanging a door upside down, but no one doubted their commitment to restoring the historic structure. Some spent hours sanding away layers of varnish accumulated over almost six decades to reveal beautiful hardwood floors. Others contributed their organizational talents—many were managers or paper-pushers in their day jobs—to keep other workers supplied with raw materials, equipment, and inspiration. The volunteers worked from seven in the morning to seven at night, occasionally pausing to talk with neighbors from the area who stopped by with snacks and lunches, but laboring like mules until there was too little light to continue. They all felt the effort was worth it every time they saw the great house standing on the corner in all its former glory.

Add parentheses as needed to the following passage.

1. Native Americans inhabited almost every region of North
    America, from the peoples farthest north the Inuit to those in the
    Southwest the Hopi, the Zuni.

2. In parts of what are now New Mexico and Colorado, during the
    thirteenth century some ancient tribes moved off the mesas no
    one knows exactly why to live in cliff dwellings.

3. One cliff dwelling at Mesa Verde covers an area of 66 meters 217
    feet by 27 meters 89 feet.

4. Spectacular as they are, the cliff dwellings served the tribes
    known as the Anasazi for only a short time.

5. The Anasazi left their cliff dwellings, possibly because of a
    prolonged drought AD 1276-1299 in the entire region.

Add and delete dashes as necessary to improve the sentences below. You may need to interchange commas and dashes.

1.   Legend has it that Beethoven's Third Symphony was dedicated to Napoleon Bonaparte the champion of French revolutionary ideals until he declared himself emperor.

2.   Scholars believe—though they can't be sure—that the symphony was initially called *Bonaparte*—testimony to just how much the idealistic Beethoven admired the French leader.

3.   The Third Symphony a revolutionary work itself is now known by the title *Eroica*.

4.   The Third, the Fifth, the Sixth, the Seventh, the Ninth Symphonies, they all contain musical passages that most people recognize immediately.

5.   The opening four notes of Beethoven's Fifth, da, da, da, da, may be the most famous in all of music.

In the following sentences, underline the preferable forms of the words in parentheses. Use a dictionary if you are not familiar with the terms.

1.   Local citizens have a (*once in a lifetime, once-in-a-lifetime*) opportunity to preserve an (*old-growth, oldgrowth*) forest.

2.   A large, wooded parcel of land is about to be turned into a shopping mall by (*real-estate, real estate*) speculators and (*pinstripe suited, pinstripe-suited*) investors.

3.   The forest provides a haven for (*wild-life, wildlife*) of all varieties, from (*great horned owls, great-horned owls*) to (*ruby throated, ruby-throated*) hummingbirds.

4.   Does any community need (*video stores, video-stores*), (*T shirt, T-shirt*) shops, and (*over priced, overpriced*) boutiques more than acres of natural habitat?

5.   This (*recently-proposed, recently proposed*) development can be stopped by a petition to the (*city-council, city council*).

Underline the boldfaced titles and names that should be italicized, and add quotation marks where they are needed. Leave unmarked those titles and names that need neither italics nor quotation marks.

1. launching a **Titan III** at Cape Kennedy

2. **My Fair Lady** playing at the **Paramount Theater**

3. watching **I Love Lucy**

4. sunk on the passenger ship **Andrea Doria**

5. returning **A Farewell to Arms** to the public library

6. playing **Casablanca** again on a **Panasonic** DVD player

7. discussing the colors of Picasso's **The Old Guitarist**

8. reading Jackson's **The Lottery** one more time

9. picking up a copy of **The Los Angeles Times**

10. whistling **Here Comes the Sun** from the Beatles' **Abbey Road**

Correct problems in capitalization in the following sentences.

1. The passenger next to me asked, "do you remember when air

    travel used to be a pleasure?"

2. I couldn't reply immediately: My tray table had just flopped open

    and hit me on the knees.

3. The plane we were on—A jumbo jet that seated nine or ten

    across—had been circling Dulles International for hours.

4. "We'll be landing momentarily," the flight attendant mumbled,

    "If we are lucky."

5. I had seen the film version of this flight: *airplane!*

Exercise 96
Capitalizing Names and Abbreviations

Capitalize names and abbreviations in the following sentences as necessary.

1.   The east asian students visiting the district of columbia were

     mostly juniors pursuing b.a.'s while the african-american students

     were predominantly graduate students seeking master's degrees.

2.   The constitution and the declaration of independence are on view

     at the national archives.

3.   I heard the doorkeeper at the hilton speaking spanish to the

     general secretary of the united nations.

4.   Visitors to washington, d.c., include people from around the

     world: russians from moscow, egyptians from cairo, aggies from

     texas, buckeyes from ohio.

5.   At the white house, the president will host a conference on

     democracy and free enterprise in the spring, probably in april.

Draw a line through boldfaced words that have faulty usage and write the correct form in the space above.

1.   That claim of **her's** may be right.

2.   **Moufidas** belief was that the main concern of most **citizens'** was

       a thriving economy.

3.   **Society's** problems today are not as great as they were in the

       1900's; each generation benefits from its **parent's** sacrifices

       while tackling **it's** own problems.

4.   **Its** a shame that people forget how much they have benefited

       from someone **elses** labor.

5.   Children are notorious for ignoring their **elders** generosity;

       ingratitude is even one of the major themes of *King Lear's* plot.

Exercise 98
Using Abbreviations

SFHB 42a
SFW 44b
SFC 37a

Correct the sentences below. Draw a line through faulty usage and, in the space above your strikeout, abbreviate where appropriate or expand abbreviations that would be incorrect in college or professional writing. Check punctuation for accuracy and consistency. If you use periods with acronyms and initialisms, use them throughout the passage.

1.   There's a better than 70% chance of rain today.

2.   Irene sent angry ltrs. to a dozen networks, including NBC,

      A.B.C., ESPN, and CNN.

3.   The Emperor Claudius was born in 10 b.c. and died in 54 A.D.

4.   Dr. Kovatch, M.D., works for the Federal Department of

      Agriculture (FDA).

5.   I owe the company only $175 dollars & expect to pay the full

      amount before the end of the mo.

Exercise 99
Using Numbers

SFHB 42b
SFW 44c
SFC 37b

Correct the sentences below. Draw a line through faulty usage and, in the space above your strikeout, change numerals to words or words to numerals as appropriate for college or professional writing. Some expressions may not need revision.

1.   4 people will be honored at the ceremony beginning at nine p.m.

2.   The culture contained more than 500,000,000,000 cells.

3.   We forgot who won the Nobel Peace Prize in nineteen ninety-

      one.

4.   The examination will include a question about the 1st, the 4th, or

      the Tenth Amendment.

5.   We paid $79.80 for the hotel room and twenty dollars for

      admission to the park.

Exercise 100
Forming Plurals

SFHB 25a
SFW 45a
SFC 20a

Write the plural forms of the boldfaced words, using the spaces above the words. Consult your handbook or dictionary if necessary.

1. The Corner Café sold typical coffeehouse beverages, including

    several different **espresso**.

2. On the walls of the café were **photo** of the local soccer team and

    their moms.

3. The decor reflected the late **1990**, sleek and jazzy.

4. With its sports **trophy** and open doors, the place reflected the

    interest of the neighborhood.

5. No one knows how many **cupful** of coffee have been served

    there.

6. Many of yesterday's soccer heroes think of themselves as

    alumnus of the Corner Café.

SAMPLE ANSWERS

In this section you will find sample answers to the first item in some of the exercises. Use them as a guide to how you can answer other items.

SHAPING LANGUAGE

Exercise 1   (possible answer)
Depending upon degree of acquaintance, the style may vary from moderately formal to slightly informal. In describing qualifications for the position, the writer might include personal details to give the reader hints about his or her personality.

Exercise 2   (no sample answer)

Exercise 3   (possible answer)
People in their 40s and 50s who want to look their best often consider cosmetic surgery.

Exercise 4   (possible answer)
The term "girls" and the assumption that female college students cannot succeed in chemistry will probably offend college women and in particular those studying chemistry.

Exercise 5   (possible answer)
"Cops" is generally perceived as a prejudicial term by the law-enforcement community.

Exercise 6   (possible answer)
Lincoln Brown. the new college president, aimed to raise $3 million to renovate the drama facilities on campus.

Exercise 7   (possible answer)
Activists from remarkably different political groups are among those who are unhappy about the lack of morality and standards in the television shows coming from Hollywood today and who would like to see pressure on producers for more responsible programming.

Exercise 8   (possible answer)
The restaurateurs protested when the city decided to increase the number of health inspectors.

Exercise 9   (possible answer)
Students everywhere traditionally dread writing research papers.

Exercise 10   (possible answer)
The job a young woman has in high school can play an important role in introducing her to new responsibilities and increasing her self-confidence. Just as important, working will accustom her to expecting to earn her own way through life. She shouldn't anticipate that someone else, usually a man, will shoulder the burden of providing her security, shelter, health care, or other necessities.

Exercise 11
Scholars disagree about Alexander the Great's ultimate military goals.

Exercise 12   (possible answer)
On the newspaper's seventy-fifth anniversary, the governor visited the editorial offices.

Exercise 13   (possible answer)
If you are near Greene County this weekend, you should visit the autumn Concours d'Elegance, an annual exhibit of classic cars.

Exercise 14   (possible answer)
The registrar's note <u>clarifies</u> the school's admissions policy.

Exercise 15   (possible answer)
Many people <u>believe</u> that the federal government has grown too large.

Exercise 16   (possible answer)
I realized that to reach law school I would have to improve my writing skills.

Exercise 17   (possible answer)
The Grand Canyon is a unique geological treasure in northwestern Arizona, formed by the relentless power of the Colorado River cutting a gorge for eons through solid rock.

Exercise 18   (possible answer)
Author Patrick O'Brian has written one of the most popular series of historical novels about the British Royal Navy during the Napoleonic Wars.

Exercise 19   (possible answer)
Some of the people <u>who</u> might be willing to endure a little less environmental consciousness are parents of children ~~whom~~ environmentalists have turned into Green Police.

Exercise 20   (no sample answer)

UNDERSTANDING GRAMMAR

Exercise 21   (possible answer)
Halloween may be the oddest **holiday** of the year.

Exercise 22
The IRS agent asked the <u>auditor</u> three tough <u>questions</u>.

Exercise 23
<u>Waving at the crowd</u>, the winner of the marathon took a victory lap. (*Adjective; modifies "winner"*)

Exercise 24
The wood on the deck <u>warped after only one summer</u>.

Exercise 25   (possible answer)
All the students in the class <u>who had nose rings and tattoos</u> said they supported the Democratic party's proposals.

Exercise 26   (possible answer)
Even though <u>most of us love to debate about politics</u>, Americans vote in record low numbers.

Exercise 27, p. 22
<u>What politicians say</u> often matters less than <u>how they say it</u>. (*subjects*)

Exercise 28   (possible answer)
The stock market finally rose, <u>but</u> investors remained nervous.

Exercise 29   (possible answer)
If I agree to read *War and Peace* by the end of the summer, then you <u>must agree to attend the film festival with me in September</u>.

Exercise 30   (possible answer)
Ordinary books are still more convenient than most computerized texts; <u>moreover,</u> they employ a technology that doesn't go out of date as quickly—paper.

Exercise 31   (possible answer)
Today, French Impressionist paintings are favorites among art lovers, <u>but</u> the public loudly rejected them at their debut in the nineteenth century.

Exercise 32   (possible answer)

Don't feel sorry for the spare and thorny plants you see in a desert; they don't want or need more water.

Exercise 33   (possible answer)

Even though we think of books as portable, bound volumes, the original books of Babylonia and Assyria were collections of inscribed clay tablets stored in labeled containers too heavy for one person to move.

Exercise 34   (possible answer)

For many years, scientists believed that there might be another planet on the fringes of the solar system whose gravitational pull influenced the orbit of Uranus. Scientists spent decades speculating about its mass, distance from earth, and orbital mechanics. However, there was no concrete evidence that this additional planet existed.

Exercise 35   (possible answer)

On opening night at the new Tex-Mex restaurant, the manager called the servers together to be sure they understood all the items on the menu, could pronounce *fajitas*, and would remember to ask "Salt or no salt?" when customers ordered margaritas.

Exercise 36   (possible answer)

Although most movie stars are human and created by the usual birds-and-bees process, one of the most popular movie stars in recent memory, the liquid metal cyborg in *Terminator 2*, was created by a computer.

Exercise 37   (no sample answer)

Exercise 38   (possible answer)

At one time the walls in many Philadelphia neighborhoods were covered with graffiti; however, they are covered with murals today.

Exercise 39   (possible answer)

Centuries of superstition and ignorance have given bats a bad reputation; millions of the flying mammals are killed each year in a misguided effort to protect livestock, crops, and people.

Exercise 40, p. 34   (possible answer)

Although among the most famous of reptiles, rattlesnakes have only recently been studied by biologists.

Exercise 41   (possible answer)
The <u>graceful, towering</u> elm trees once common throughout North America have disappeared, victims of <u>Dutch-elm</u> disease.

Exercise 42   (possible answer)
Lisa and Julia wanted to find a women's group that was politically sophisticated and that could help them plan their strategy for lobbying.

Exercise 43
confident

Exercise 44   (possible answer)
Ms. Oliveras was disappointed with the grant proposals she read–she thought the projects they proposed should have been ~~more~~ unique.

Exercise 45   (possible answer)
<u>Sadly</u>, the elm trees once <u>quite</u> common throughout North America have <u>almost completely</u> disappeared.

Exercise 46
People who regularly attend the theater complain that the manners of the average audience members are in severe decline.

Exercise 47   (possible answer)
Some critics claim that in this age of videos, computers, and the Internet, young people ~~don't~~ hardly read anymore.

Exercise 48
more

Exercise 49
continue

Exercise 50
are

Exercise 51
reports; are

Exercise 52
embrace

Exercise 53
strides

Exercise 54
will rule

Exercise 55
spoken

Exercise 56, p. 47
<u>have been bitten</u>   (no change)

Exercise 57
be

Exercise 58   (possible answer)
Leah avidly read about gardening, although she had never planted <u>a garden</u>
herself.

Exercise 59   (possible answer)
Amanda could hardly believe that the representatives from Habitat for Humanity
would visit Madison, Wisconsin, when <u>the weather</u> was so bad.   (*Replaces
ambiguous "it"*)

Exercise 60
Even tourists just visiting the building soon noticed the aging state capitol's
sagging floors, unreliable plumbing, and exposed electrical conduits–<u>all of
which</u> was embarrassing.

Exercise 61   (possible answer)
Many college classes are conducted using the Socratic method, but they aren't
always successful.

Exercise 62
their; its

Exercise 63
he or she is

Exercise 64
their (*agrees with "customers"*)

Exercise 65
she

Exercise 66
who

Exercise 67
she

Exercise 68
he

Exercise 69
It's

Exercise 70
There is usually not much doubt about who's responsible for enormous
environmental disasters.

Exercise 71
who

Exercise 72
dream; happens

Exercise 73
have had

Exercise 74
have been talking

Exercise 75, p. 61
Before I studied psychology, I (had) thought it was an easy subject.

Exercise 76
must *or* should

Exercise 77
Megan's boss told her, "You had better ~~to~~ improve your attitude, or we will have
to take disciplinary action."

Exercise 78
NC

Exercise 79
Many people have visited the new restaurant downtown called Rock-and-Roll
Hamburger Haven.

UNDERSTANDING PUNCTUATION AND MECHANICS

Exercise 80
Hannibal simply outfoxed the Roman general Varro at Cannae.

Exercise 81
When Mount Saint Helens erupted in 1980, the north slope collapsed, sending torrents of mud and rock down into the Toutle River valley.

Exercise 82
Carter, a sales clerk with a passion for Native American art, urged Iona, his manager at a gallery in Alpine, to increase her stock of Navajo rugs.

Exercise 83
Sentence is correct.

Exercise 84
Psychologists / who have studied moods / say that such emotional states are contagious / and compare them to social viruses.

Exercise 85
In the autumn of 1863, Abraham Lincoln, President of the United States, traveled to Gettysburg, Pennsylvania, to speak at the dedication of a cemetery there.

Exercise 86
For many years, biblical spectacles were a staple of the Hollywood film industry; however, in recent years few such films have been produced.

Exercise 87   (possible answer)
The action in mad-killer movies like *Scream* follows a predictable pattern: A masked killer dispatches random teenagers and even an occasional high school principal; attacks the annoying reporter, Gale Weathers; and attacks and, maybe, kills Dewey, the bumbling cop.

Exercise 88
No one ever forgets the conclusion of Hitchcock's *Psycho*: the discovery of Norman's mother in the rocking chair.

Exercise 89
Much to the tourists' surprise, their uproar over conditions at their so-called "luxury resort" attracted the attention of a local television station.

Exercise 90   (no sample answer)

Exercise 91
Native Americans inhabited almost every region of North America, from the people farthest north (the Inuit) to those in the Southwest (the Hopi, the Zuni).

Exercise 92
Legend has it that Beethoven's Third Symphony was dedicated to Napoleon Bonaparte—the champion of French revolutionary ideals until he declared himself emperor.

Exercise 93
once-in-a-lifetime; old-growth

Exercise 94
Titan III

Exercise 95
The passenger next to me asked, "<u>Do</u> you remember when air travel used to be a pleasure?"

Exercise 96
The <u>E</u>ast <u>A</u>sian students visiting the <u>D</u>istrict of <u>C</u>olumbia were mostly juniors pursuing <u>B.A.'s</u> while the <u>A</u>frican-<u>A</u>merican students were predominantly graduate students seeking master's degrees.

Exercise 97
hers

Exercise 98
There's a better than 70 <u>percent</u> chance of rain today.

Exercise 99
<u>Four</u> people will be honored at the ceremony beginning at <u>9:00</u> p.m.

Exercise 100
espressos